When Tomorrow Never Comes

T.M. Workman

Table of Contents

Watching my mom overcome the stresses of life gives me the confidence to face whatever the world throws at me.

- Chloe Ann Marie

CHAPTER
One

Ain't No Sunshine When She's Gone

In the quiet suburb of Worthington Hills in Louisville, Kentucky lived a vibrant 32-year-old woman named Gail Ann Robinson. She was a dedicated and passionate elementary school teacher, adored by her students, and respected by her colleagues. However, behind her cheerful facade, Gail Ann carried the weight of a crumbling marriage. For nearly eight months, she was estranged from her husband and my dad: Thomas. Then, their relationship took a dark and tumultuous turn.

It was a cold winter morning in Louisville, and like any other day my mom dropped off me and my sister at daycare and headed to work. But it wasn't any other day. It was the last day we would hear our mother's voice, the last day she would tell us to get dressed, and the last day she would tell us she loved us. It was the first of many lasts.

Our mom was a second grade teacher at Englehard Elementary (about ten miles away from my school), but she never made it to work that day. In fact, she didn't even get out of her car to walk us to the door of the daycare as she did every day since we started going to an in-home daycare near our house several years prior.

Our daycare lady was a sweet, Christian woman who stood about five feet tall with soft wispy hair and fluffy arms for a warm embrace. She had a gentle strength about her and you always felt the love radiate from her being. She followed her purpose as a daycare provider. Unbeknownst to her, her daycare provided a place of refuge, peace, and safety for me and my sister.

My dad was the first boy in a family of twelve children (two boys and ten girls). Yes, ten girls!! Eight children were born in Charleston, West Virginia. The other four children were born in Cincinnati, Ohio, eventually settling in the projects of Lincoln Heights, Ohio.

Lincoln Heights was the largest all Black community in the United States located just north of Cincinnati. It wasn't quite a suburb, but it wasn't the city either. Some would describe Lincoln Heights as the valley, zone 15, the country little village north of the city.

As the oldest, my dad had a lot of pressure to do things for his siblings. He wanted to give them a better life, so he started working at a very young age. Although he loved his sisters, their relationship was a bit dysfunctional because he would fight with them like anybody else. After all, he was outnumbered in a house full of girls and a disabled mother. His mother had Multiple Sclerosis (MS) and his father, my grandfather, was rumored to have pushed her down the steps resulting in her never walking again. Needless to say, my dad's childhood was far from ideal.

My dad met my mom when he was the ripe age of fourteen or fifteen. He fought with my mom as he did with his sisters. My mom's family situation wasn't much better. She never established a relationship with her father and was raised by her maternal grandparents and extended family, including a stepfather who tried to touch her inappropriately. She immediately told her mother, despite him offering her hush money to keep quiet. Her mother put the stepfather out of the house and divorced him once she found out.

My dad loved my mom. He wanted to protect her, but at the same time their relationship was toxic. My mom was a pretty woman with dark chocolate skin and a coke bottle frame. She was charming to men. However, she dealt with some insecurities because of colorism with people in the community. This was due to having a darker complexion than her siblings. She was very talented, a social butterfly, and had a beautiful smile like her father. She enjoyed interacting with people and loved to be the center of attention and she got plenty of it as the first born. She loved to dance and was the life of the party! My dad would get jealous of how much attention she would get and lash out. They fought for years and their relationship continued until she left for college where she became a member of Delta Sigma Theta Sorority, Incorporated.

My dad joined the army and then married another young lady, but as fate would have it, old habits die hard. My dad ran into my mom one time when she was home visiting from college and the sparks were reignited like they never left. My dad was separated from his wife. Before long, he was divorced and made a family with Gail Ann, his childhood sweetheart.

My mom's mother was not too keen on them rekindling their relationship because it was not a healthy situation. While domestic violence was common during those times, it was taboo to discuss it openly.

My dad was a short man but for whatever he lacked in height, he made up for it in personality. His personality was larger than life! He was one of the most charming men I knew, and he could finesse the best of them. He was attractive, athletic, and had a great sense of humor. He was an athlete in college so over time he became a master at getting people to do what he wanted.

My mom was no exception to my dad's need to control, but my mom couldn't be controlled. She was a first-generation college graduate from Kentucky State University and she came from a long line of strong Black women. Shortly after reconnecting, my mom and dad were back to the makeup to breakup relation-ship they had known for so many years. That toxicity set the events of my mom's death in motion.

The day before my mom passed was my third birthday celebration. It was complete with cake, balloons, presents, family, and friends all gathered at our house in Louisville on Luray Court. This was the house my mom and dad shared before they separated for the last time about eight months prior. Supposedly, my mom's boyfriend gifted me a pair of Smurf roller skates for my birthday and my dad was upset about it.

My parents fought that night like they did so many times before, but this fight was different, leaving destruction in its wake. Broken glass, walls filled with holes, and household items turned weapons, spewed about the once pristine house my mom now shared with me and my sister. While my dad was willing to let us live in the house, the car was something different. My mom drove a late 70s model Lincoln Town car but when they separated, he took the car leaving my mom without transportation. He was out enjoying his life and how we got around was the least of his worries. As the saying goes, "How you get them is how you lose them." His new girlfriend was the apple of my dad's eye, which meant my mom and us kids were becoming a bit of a burden for my dad who liked to control things.

Without a car, my mom went and got her old VW Bug out of storage, had it serviced, and was on the road again. It was a tiny little car, shiny, blue with white interior and chrome accents. Unfortunately, it was far from what she was accustomed to with the Lincoln Town car.

The morning of Nov 11, 1983 was rainy, and my mom was in a hurry to get to work. In her haste to get to school and desperation to cover her battle wounds, she crossed the center line of the two-lane road and hit the pick-up truck on the other side head on. She covered a black eye with her makeup compact to ensure no one learned of her turbulent relationship with her estranged husband. After all, they had broken up so many times before. Surely, they would be back together, eventually. This time she had baggage, she had kids, so things wouldn't be quite the same. After the accident, there were several first responders on the scene to tend to those injured. Unfortunately, my mother was the only one with life threatening injuries; although three other people were injured because of the accident. My mom was in critical condition for four days at Humana Hospital University with multiple injuries after being pinned in her car. Police said no charges were filed.

It took hours to get my father to the hospital after the accident. My mother's family had to put out an APB on the radio for him to finally arrive at the hospital with a preacher by his side. My dad was for all intents and purposes the next of kin, so he would have the authority to decide when to pull the life support. And ultimately, he would be the one planning her funeral with the help of A.D. Porter & Sons Funeral Home on Chestnut St. in the West End of Louisville, Kentucky. After the funeral in Louisville, there was a second funeral in my mom's hometown of Cincinnati, Ohio. Her body was eventually airlifted and buried in Spring Grove Cemetery in Cincinnati, Ohio with an open plot next to her for my dad once he passed.

It's crazy how life works. When my dad died 34 years later, he was buried in a veteran cemetery in Dayton, Ohio because he spent his final days living in northern Ohio near Cleveland. To this day, there is still an open plot paid for many years prior for someone else to occupy next to Gail Ann: beloved wife, mother, teacher, and friend. For as long as I can remember, my mother would show herself to me as a white butterfly. She would come during sad times, happy times, and times when she knew I just needed a friend. For about two weeks after my father passed, two butterflies appeared and then one day they stopped, and it went back to just one. My theory is that my mom welcomed my dad into heaven and later told him he was on his own! She was like that. Even on her worse days, she would help in whatever way she could. Ain't no sunshine when she's gone, but there is always a butterfly to remind you of her beautiful smile on any given day, rain or shine.

My mom's voice was silenced the day she passed and her light dimmed. I hope that her spirit can live on through the pages of this book. And someone will be inspired to fight, someone will be inspired to keep going, someone will be inspired to run, and someone will be inspired to live to see another day. My mom said she would get help for her domestic violence issues on Monday. Her accident was on Friday, but the days leading up to her death were anything but peace on earth. You recall me talking about the black eye, but the police report didn't mention anything of the sort. She was in a car accident so why would there be a need to do an investigation? There were several witnesses that saw her crash into the red and white pick-up truck. The road conditions were bad and the curvy road on which the accident took place was a dangerous thoroughfare. It was an accident. Or was it?

This was a question I asked myself for years growing up, but how would I ever know the truth? My dad would certainly never tell me what exactly took place those days leading up to my mom's death. Who else might know? Who else would be willing to open Pandora's box for the sake of giving my mom a voice? We shall see...

CHAPTER Two

The Struggle Within

Gail was always a strong-willed woman, but her failing marriage left her emotionally vulnerable. As the days passed, the strain of her personal life seeped into her professional one, and Gail found it increasingly challenging to maintain her usual composure at work.

Her friends and family saw the toll it was taking on her, but Gail was fiercely independent and refused to burden them with her problems. She sought solace in her students, poured her heart and soul into her teaching, and found some relief in the joy they brought her. She confided in one of her close friends and fellow teacher about seeking help for her domestic violence situation the Monday after the accident took place. On the Tuesday following the accident, my dad, her estranged husband, made the decision to pull the plug on her life support. My mom was so badly injured in the accident that when I went to see her in the hospital, I threw up at the sight of her bruised and battered body. She lied in the hospital bed with tubes coming from everywhere and to my three-year-old self, she was unrecognizable. After my initial response to seeing her, I was not permitted back into the hospital room. That was the last time I saw my mother "alive" although she was brain dead from the impact of the collision. My sister and I attended the funeral, but I was too young to remember most of the details. My sister was three years older than me so her memories were typically a little more vivid.

Recently, I asked my sister what she remembered from the days leading up to my birthday party and our mother's accident. She recalled my birthday party being small with just a few family members and friends at our home. We all wore mouse ears so perhaps it was a Minnie Mouse themed birthday party with a cake featuring my name and some balloons. She remembered me getting some Smurf skates, some clothes and other toys as birthday gifts from various people. When I asked her what stood out about the morning of the accident, she mentioned that while she didn't see our dad at the daycare, she could feel he was there. That morning, my sister was fearful because she broke up the fight between our parents the night before. She told me the fight was bad with broken glass everywhere and how shook up she was because of the altercation. From her perspective, it was a bad fight and it went on until around 10 p.m. She assumed they would play hooky the next day from school and work because she overheard our mother talking to her friend, colleague, and former roommate about not going to school the next day. To my sister's surprise, our mother hopped out the bed that morning and started getting dressed to go to work. She assumed it was simply because she was so dedicated to her job and her students.

Obviously, none of us will ever truly know what happened that cold winter morning but I asked my sister what she thought happened. She said, "I think daddy went into a rage and mowed her down with his car." I asked several times what she meant but she kept repeating the same thing, "I think he mowed her down with that big Lincoln." I agree that is likely what happened, although I would describe it more like chasing her down with his car. I witnessed my dad when he was in a rage. He could be very menacing; and his wrath was scary, ominous even. I recall a situation when I was about five or six years old, and my dad and my stepmother were arguing. My stepmother was the only mother that I remembered, and she was good to me and my sister. So when my dad was screaming and hollering and eventually hitting her, our natural reaction was to run with her outside. After all, she was our "mother." She cared for us, tended to our every need, cooked for us, and kept a roof over our head when our dad was "away." In his moment of rage, something clicked in his head and he chased us all down with his car, turning every way with no regard for human life. We ran in different directions to avoid being hit by his car. He screamed, "I'm ya daddy!" "You wanna go with her?" We continued to run and cry until finally the terror stopped, just as quickly as it began.

When I look at the pictures from my mother's accident and see how the cars were thrown about like toy trucks, I can't help but flash back to that day my dad chased us in a fit of rage. Was that what our mother experienced that morning? Did she see my dad coming full speed in a Lincoln Town car at her little VW Bug as she made her way up the winding road to Englehard Elementary? Did anyone else witness what took place? If so, are they still alive to talk about it? Would they come forward with that information? There are so many questions from that fateful day. Who knows if any of them will ever be answered but for the sake of my mother's legacy, I will try to find as many answers as I can.

While most of my sister's memories are rich with details, she vaguely remembers being at the hospital the day following the accident. I think she blocked those memories considering they were traumatic for a five year old. One thing she seems adamant about is the recount of us going back to the house on Luray Court several years later. She mentioned that something happened at the house on Brad Court; and suddenly, we had to move back to the house on Luray. My dad and stepmother were renting the house on Brad Court, so I am not sure if the owners needed the house back or what took place. My biological mom and dad owned the house on Luray Court. I assume the mortgage was paid in full with the life insurance from my mother's death benefit.

My sister remembers the house on Luray Court being completely remodeled while they were living there and how our mother's things were discarded to make way for the newly remodeled space, eliminating any trace of our mother's memory. The wallpaper was removed, mirrors taken down, all décor completely reimagined, and the walls repainted to prepare for a new life at Luray Court sans Gail Ann. Before I can take you into the new life and what it would all entail, I would be remiss not to give you the account of my other cousins that came to the house from Cincinnati that day to show care and concern for my beautiful mother, Gail. My mother's side of the family was extremely close so when you saw one of them, you generally saw them all. Traveling from Cincinnati was my grandmother (Nana), likely my mother's two sisters (Sybil and Crystal), my mother's brother (Keith), his wife (Maria), their two sons (Keith and Steven), my grandmother's sisters (Aunt Marilyn and Aunt Peggy) and perhaps a few other cousins Kelvin, Joyce, Bruce, Jimmy, and Maurice (my great aunt's children).

According to one of my cousins, when they arrived at our house in Louisville, the house was in shambles with busted door jams. The door to the main bedroom appeared to be broken as if someone forced their way in. He mentioned everyone from Cincinnati stayed for a few days at the house on Luray Court and that most of them went to visit my mother at the hospital. Unfortunately, everyone was not allowed to enter the hospital room due to facility restrictions. He noted that everyone was very upset and tempers were high at the hospital. At one point, my Uncle Keith approached my dad for answers of which I am not sure he ever received. Naturally, my mom's family wanted to know what happened. They wondered how my mom was pinned in her tiny Volkswagen the day after my parents had fought like animals, leaving my mother with a black eye, and now brain dead in a hospital bed. We all wanted answers, we desperately needed answers. Answers we may never receive.

CHAPTER
Three

Childhood Trauma & The Aftermath

As I noted earlier in the book, I celebrated my third birthday the day before my mother's car accident and my sister was only five years old. I have an eight-year-old daughter so the best reflection I can use to compare to is how she was at three and five. My daughter has very minimal memories of the things I remember about her at three. She was a sassy little three year old and I called them the terrible threes! In contrast, from what I could gather about myself at that age, I was pretty quiet and a bit reserved. My guess is losing my mother, the one person sent to love and protect me, made me a bit uncertain about the world and who I could or should trust. I think those experiences contributed to some of my childhood trauma. It is very difficult for me to trust people even to this day. If someone says they are going to do something, I believe it when I see it. Just telling me something has absolutely no bearing on what I expect will happen. For as long as I could remember, I was a bedwetter. If I visited someone's house and spent the night, there was an extremely high likelihood I was going to wet the bed. Adults could cut off fluids, make me use the bathroom before I laid down, or wake me up in the middle of the night to use the potty. Nothing worked! It did not matter what you did, I was still going to pee on myself that night and lay in it as if it was the warmest, most secure place I had ever been. I would warn people that they should put some plastic down on the bed because I had zero control once I was asleep. Looking back, I wonder if wetting the bed was another part of the trauma I experienced from the passing of my mother. I also feared getting out of the bed in the middle of the night because my parents fought in the dark or Perhaps laying in a sea of my own urine was somehow therapeutic for me. It was familiar, it represented a safe place for me to lay, and if I was dreaming I wouldn't have to wake up to the nightmare of living here on this earth without my mom guiding and protecting me. I didn't stop peeing in the bed until I was like ten years old. Coincidently, that was the same year my sister and I moved to Cincinnati to live with our maternal grandmother. I lived in a world of uncertainty. My mother passed. My father was there, but there was always an unspoken wrath to avoid with him. As the younger child, I had my sister's actions to look to as what not to do. My sister experienced the bulk of the wrath from our father. She was the oldest, she knew better, and she was the big sister. For years, I never really understood why my sister and I were so different. We were raised in the same households from birth to eighteen. We lived with our parents until I was three and she was five. Then, we lived with our dad and stepmother from three and five until about seven and nine. Lastly, we lived with my mother's mother(my nana) at the ages of ten and thirteen.

When I was in college, I was introduced to the book, "Heal Your Body," by Louise Hay. It outlines emotional and mental causes of illness. Bedwetting is highlighted with the cause, "Fear of parent, usually the Father." During the early part of my childhood, abuse and fighting between my parents were commonplace. When I was doing interviews for this book, my cousin told me a story about an early memory he had of the months following my mother's death. Evidently, I fell asleep in my Aunt Maria's brand-new car and when I awoke I urinated on myself. He recalled me being hysterical about it, saying how sorry I was to my aunt. She reassured me that it was okay, and she would clean it up. That story served as a bit of a confirmation that I may have been met with my dad's wrath whenever I had an accident and that may have contributed to my continuous bedwetting until long after my sister and I were removed from our dad's care.

When I think back on how traumatic events impact kids, it seems to be more detrimental to the child if they are at an impressionable age. In my opinion, five is an extremely impressionable age and so is thirteen. At five, most children are transitioning from daycare to school potentially. They are beginning to understand that everyone is not their friend and really starting to grasp the concept that the world is full of ups and downs that you may or may not have any say over. At thirteen, many are going through puberty or may have just experienced puberty and everything that they once knew changed. As a child, I didn't give these ideas much thought. As an adult, I can't help but think they had an impact on the differences between my perspective of the world and my sister's perspective of the world.

While my mother passed on, my first memory of having a mother was actually with my step mother, Bernita . It was a traumatic memory, but my first vivid memory. My sister and I were mourning the loss of our mom. We seemed to always come together as a united front to express our grievances and to cry about the unfairness of life. On this day, we were upset with my stepmother and sad about our mom no longer being there. I believe it was the December after the car accident because we just finished watching the movie, Frosty the Snowman. We expressed our discontent to our father and he lashed out at us saying, "Your mother is gone! Bernita is going to be your new mother!" "You all need to get used to it and call her mom from here on out!" As a child, it hit hard. When I think back on it as an adult, it was even more painful to witness. Those words made me think it's not okay to cry! Your time for mourning is over. Accept that your mother is gone and move on with your life. As a small child, that is exactly what I did. My sister might have unpacked those words much differently. Forget about the woman: with whom you experienced your first milestones; who taught you how to walk and talk; who protected you when the world seemed crazy and from the father who was supposed to be a protector was wailing on her and all you wanted to do was protect her. Forget about the woman that carried you in her womb for nine months and almost died giving birth to you due to toxemia. Forget about her, here is your replacement. Her name is Bernita and you will call her "mom."

I had several therapy sessions, but I never talked to my therapist about this situation. I think it was the blocking out of any memories of my birth mom that made my childhood so idyllic. If I had to guess how that experience impacted me as it relates to childhood trauma, I guess it is the primary reason I don't spend too much time sulking, healing or the like. I experience the painful event, deal with my emotions, and move on. It's not like I don't remember painful events. I simply have a coping mechanism that allows me to deal with them, process my emotions related to said event, and move on. I am not sure if that is good or bad, it just is. At the age of ten or eleven, the last memory that I think contributed to my childhood trauma was losing my dad to a new family. My dad met this woman and she had two little girls about the same age as me and my sister. We moved to Cincinnati to live with our maternal grandmother and they moved into our old rooms. It was like he removed us from the story and replaced us with a new woman and two new daughters to boot. We went back to Louisville to visit and they were staying in our rooms, wearing our clothes, and sleeping in our beds! Mind you, mine was rotting with piss from all those years of wetting the bed so I wasn't the least bit bothered. She could have that little pissy bed as far as I was concerned. I was bothered because it felt like my dad sought to replace us. He dropped new children into his life and continued as if nothing changed.

My best guess is that my experience with my dad replacing me and my sister with his girlfriend's kids gave me abandonment issues. If things didn't work out, you could be replaced. People were replaceable. No one was exempt. The way this shows up in my life today is that I am always waiting for the other foot to drop. I need to leave you before you decide to leave me. If things aren't working, I don't ever have a problem leaving. Because after all, people are replaceable. Just find someone else and put them in the other person's shoes. It will be fine. The only problem is, it never really is fine. It might suffice for the moment, but eventually there will be someone that is not replaceable. I hope this book helps you identify when you've met the one that is not meant to be replaced. The one that was sent into your life to protect and provide in a way that you never knew was even possible.

CHAPTER
Four

Self-Reflection

This chapter is here to help you take a trip down memory lane; to give you a chance to reflect on your childhood and things that may contribute to your own childhood trauma.

What is your first traumatic memory as a child?

_____

_____

_____

_____

_____

_____

_____

_____

_____

_____

_____

How did that experience impact you?

_____

_____

_____

_____

_____

_____

_____

_____

_____

How did you deal with the situation?

_____

_____

_____

_____

_____

_____

_____

_____

_____

_____

_____

_____

_____

_____

_____

_____

_____

What stands out to you the most about that situation?

_____

_____

_____

_____

_____

_____

_____

_____

_____

_____

_____

_____

_____

_____

_____

_____

_____

Do you recognize various coping mechanisms that you may have picked up because of your childhood trauma?

_____

_____

_____

_____

_____

_____

_____

_____

_____

_____

_____

_____

_____

_____

_____

CHAPTER
Five

How I Survived

People that witnessed me and my sister growing up without our mother responded in various ways. Some looked at us in pity. Some reached out to help in whatever way they could. Some stayed silent because they simply couldn't relate and did not know how to provide solace for such a grim situation. What helped me cope with the loss of my mother the most was my relationship with God. I felt that God was a mother to the motherless, a father to the fatherless. At some point, I was introduced to that scripture (Isaiah 66:12-13) and I held fast to that word. When no one was there for me in the physical, God was ALWAYS there! Over the years, I began to lean on God for whatever I needed, and He would always supply my needs. I got to a point where I would not make any major decisions without praying and asking God what He would have me to do. After all, no one was as loyal to me as He was. Why would I trust anyone else? In addition to my relationship with God, I also had a host of family members, including: my grandmother, my stepmother, aunts, and cousins that were constantly available to make me feel loved and protected. I am not sure where I would be if it were not for family, friends, and neighbors in the community that showed up to help in various ways.

As I got older, I realized the importance of a community of people. Community is not just blood relatives, but people who witness your loss firsthand and want to offer resources to lighten the load. As I had additional life experiences, I started to notice that my situation was not that dire. I mean, I didn't have my mother here on earth but if I ever needed to talk to her, she was always there in spirit. I had a stepmother who was very active in my life and later a grandmother who nurtured and guided me the best way she knew how. I had a village! What I noticed as I continued my journey is that everyone did not have a village; and my village made a difference for me. We always think our situation is as bad until we look around, hear a few other stories, and live a little. We realize our situation is not that bad. When I graduated from college, I worked at a back on track school in the West End of Cincinnati. Prior to taking the job at the school, I called my aunt to ask her what she thought about the transition. As expected, she advised against me going down to the West End because it was a rough part of town. Against her guidance, I decided to go anyway! It was the best decision I ever made for my career. I met some of the best young people and established lifelong relationships with them. I also learned through that experience that my situation was not so bad after all. Some of my students had real stories to tell. They had grandmothers running brothels, they were pimped out by their mothers, and they contracted sexually transmitted diseases from their mothers' pimps. All of this took place before the students were fourteen years old. I learned quickly how important it was not to feel sorry for myself because there was always someone with a story that would trump yours on your worst day. That brings me to the life lessons I will share with you in the next few chapters.

Lesson #1: *Stop feeling sorry for yourself*

Lesson#2: *Trust God*

Lesson #3: *Turn your pain into purpose*

CHAPTER
Six

The Power of Perspective: Beyond Self-Pity

In our journey through life, it's easy to get tangled in the web of our own troubles, convinced that our burdens are the heaviest to bear. We fall into the trap of self-pity, believing that no one could understand the weight we carry. But in the vast tapestry of human experiences, there's a crucial lesson to learn: the power of perspective.

At times, it seems as if our struggles are unique, isolating us from the world. Yet, it's in these moments that we must remind ourselves: there are billions of lives, each weaving its own tale of hardship and resilience.

Comparing our hardships to those of others isn't about belittling our own struggles. It's about acknowledging the immense spectrum of human experiences. It's recognizing that while our problems are real, they exist within a larger context. There's always someone facing battles we may never comprehend—someone grappling with adversities far beyond our own.

The antidote to self-pity lies in cultivating gratitude. It's not about disregarding our challenges, but about acknowledging the blessings amidst the storm. Take a moment each day to count your blessings, no matter how small they seem. Gratitude illuminates the path through the darkness, allowing us to see beyond our immediate hardships.

Understanding the struggles of others doesn't diminish our own, it amplifies our capacity for empathy. Engage with diverse narratives, listen to stories different from your own. It's through this connection that the walls of self-pity crumble; replaced by a profound understanding that while our battles differ, our emotions resonate universally.

Instead of succumbing to the quagmire of self-pity, channel your energy into action. Identify what's within your control and take steps toward solutions. Actively seek support from friends, mentors, or professionals. Empower yourself by acknowledging that while the situation might be tough, your capacity for resilience is boundless.

Resilience isn't about evading hardships; it's about confronting them with an unwavering spirit. Train your mind to see challenges as opportunities for growth. Every obstacle becomes a stepping stone toward greater strength and understanding. Cultivate a mindset that thrives not despite adversity, but because of it.

In the broad expanse of existence, our struggles are but a fragment of the human experience. By reframing our perspective, cultivating gratitude, fostering empathy, and taking proactive steps, we transcend the confines of self-pity. Remember, there's always someone navigating challenges beyond our imagination, urging us to find solace in our shared humanity.

Shifting the Focus

It's natural to get absorbed in our own trials and tribulations, but this mindset often leads to a distorted view of reality. Acknowledging that there are individuals enduring circumstances far more arduous than ours broadens our perspective. It redirects our focus from an inward spiral of self-pity to an outward recognition of the diverse challenges humanity faces.

Fostering Gratitude

When we immerse ourselves in an attitude of gratitude, acknowledging the things we often take for granted, it becomes a catalyst for a positive shift in perspective. Gratitude doesn't negate our hardships; it simply balances our perception, enabling us to appreciate the blessings amid the challenges.

Empathy: A Bridge to Understanding

Engaging with stories and experiences different from our own fosters empathy. It allows us to walk into someone else's shoes, even if only for a moment. This empathy doesn't invalidate our struggles; instead, it broadens our emotional spectrum, creating a deeper understanding of the diverse human condition.

Shared Humanity

Recognizing that our experiences, though unique, are part of a collective human tapestry is a powerful realization. It cultivates a sense of solidarity. It reminds us that despite our individual challenges, we are all interconnected, sharing similar emotions, hopes and fears.

Action Over Despair

Rather than being paralyzed by self-pity, acknowledging the existence of greater hardships can propel us into action. It prompts us to assess our situations, identify actionable steps, and seek support. This proactive approach empowers us, reminding us that while challenges are real, so is our capacity to overcome them.

Resilience Through Perspective

Embracing the concept that our struggles aren't isolated incidents, but part of a larger narrative of human resilience instills a resilient mindset. Every obstacle becomes an opportunity for growth, a chance to fortify our resilience and adaptability.

I first learned about resilience at the age of eleven during a school shopping experience with my nana. This was the first time going school shopping with her. Nana was on a fixed income and she took every opportunity to remind us kids of that fact. She would say, "Whoa!!! I'm on a fixed income, I can't afford that!!"

This particular day, a school friend joined us for shoe shopping. She was one of my best friends; we established a partnership because we both lost our mothers at such a young age. She lived with her aunt and her aunt sent money for her to get some shoes. In the store, we get to the section for the K-Swiss and I'm looking at the leather K-Swiss because the canvas ones get dirty too quick. My friend looked at the leather ones too, but she only had enough money for the canvas ones. My grandmother noticed the difference in the cost of the shoes and offered to pay the difference for my friend to get the leather K-Swiss. Of course, I wouldn't want to get the leather ones and she has to get the canvas ones. Unfortunately, my grandmother already did the math. She got the leather ones for my friend so I had to get the canvas ones.

I can't say I wasn't upset because the canvas ones were always so hard to keep clean! However, I couldn't wallow in disappointment because I knew my grandmother made sacrifices to get me things. There were many times when my grandmother just didn't have it. There were kids at school with all the latest everything and then there was me. We were living in poverty by the world's standards, but we never went without. There was always food to eat and we had everything we needed. As I got older, I decided I would go out and work to get the things I wanted. At age fourteen, I got my first job at McDonald's. Every day, they would ask me for my work permit; every day, I would tell them I would bring it tomorrow. When I turned sixteen, I left McDonald's and became a Loan Officer's Assistant making $16 an hour. At that point, I could buy whatever I wanted from designer bags to the latest gym shoes. Once I could afford to buy things on my own, I recognized the value of a dollar and suddenly designer things weren't really that important anymore. Looking back, there were people in our school district from all walks of life. From the poorest of the poor to the richest of the rich. We probably fell somewhere at the upper end of the poor. However, at eleven, it was hard to consider that there were levels to poverty. I could have let being poor keep me from seeing who God called me to be. I could have used my circumstances as an excuse to rob, steal, and cheat to get ahead. I was very fortunate to have my grandmother, my aunts and my great grandmother to show me what it looked like to be resilient. To recognize, when life gives you lemons, it's up to you to make homemade lemonade. And that's exactly what I did!

Conclusion

The power of perspective doesn't minimize our own challenges or dismiss our emotions. It's about acknowledging that within the vast fabric of human experiences, our struggles coexist with a myriad of others. Everyone faces their own battles. This awareness doesn't invalidate our feelings, but enriches our emotional landscape. It's an invitation to navigate our challenges with compassion, gratitude, and proactive resilience. By recognizing that there's always someone facing greater adversities, we discover strength in solidarity and hope in our shared humanity.

CHAPTER
Seven

Trusting the Divine Plan

In the labyrinth of life, where uncertainties lurk around every corner, there exists a profound solace in trusting a higher power. For many, this trust finds its anchor in a belief in God—a force that transcends the chaos and provides a semblance of order and guidance.

The Essence of Trust

Trusting in God isn't merely relying on a celestial intervention to solve life's puzzles. It's about surrendering to a belief in a divine plan, a greater purpose beyond our comprehension. It's an act of releasing control; understanding that amidst the turbulence, there's a force steering the course of our lives.

Navigating Uncertainty

Life unfolds in unpredictable ways, often diverging from the paths we meticulously plan. Our trust in God doesn't shield us from uncertainties; rather, it equips us with the resilience to weather storms, knowing that even in chaos, there's an underlying order guided by a higher wisdom.

Finding Strength in Surrender

Surrendering to a divine presence doesn't imply passivity. It's a harmonious blend of action and faith. It's about taking deliberate steps while embracing the understanding that outcomes are beyond our complete control. Trust becomes the anchor that steadies us through life's tumultuous seas.

Embracing Patience and Acceptance

When we trust God, it nurtures patience—a virtue often tested when faced with adversities. It's an acknowledgment that certain aspects of life unfold in their own time, according to a grander design. Acceptance blossoms from this patience, allowing us to embrace the present moment without resenting what's beyond our influence.

Faith in the Face of Challenges

Challenges test the fabric of our faith. In these moments, trust in God becomes an unwavering pillar, offering solace and resilience. It's during these trials that our faith deepens, strengthening our resolve to persevere, and confident that there's a purpose behind every struggle.

Seeking Guidance and Gratitude

Trusting God isn't a solitary journey. It's about seeking guidance through prayer, meditation, or seeking wisdom from sacred texts. Gratitude becomes a cornerstone, recognizing the blessings woven into the tapestry of our lives, even amidst trials.

Trusting God in Harmony with Self

Balancing trust in a higher power with personal responsibility creates harmony. It's about making decisions while seeking guidance, understanding that our actions align with a divine plan. This balance ensures that while we trust in God, we also actively participate in shaping our destinies.

Trusting in a higher power, often embodied as trusting in God, transcends a mere belief system; it's a profound philosophy that profoundly influences one's perspective and approach to life.

Trusting Beyond the Visible

1. Embracing the Unseen

Trusting in God or a higher power is rooted in acknowledging the existence of a force beyond our immediate understanding. It's about finding comfort in the unseen, knowing that there's a divine presence guiding the intricate dance of the universe.

2. Navigating Life's Complexity:

Life's journey is a tapestry woven with threads of joy, sorrow, success, and failure. Because you trust in God that does not grant you immunity from hardships, but provides the strength to navigate these complexities. It's a lighthouse guiding us through the storms, illuminating a path when darkness seems overwhelming.

Surrendering to a Greater Plan

3. Surrendering Control

Having faith in God involves relinquishing the illusion of absolute control. It's an acknowledgment that while we make choices and take actions; the ultimate outcome rests in a larger design. Surrender becomes a profound act of humility and trust in a plan beyond our finite comprehension.

4. Finding Peace in Uncertainty

Life often unfolds in ways unforeseen. Trust in the universe or a higher power nurtures an inner peace, fostering resilience in the face of uncertainties. It's an understanding that even amidst chaos, there's an underlying order, a divine orchestration guiding our paths.

Faith Amidst Trials

5. Strength in Adversity

Challenges test the resilience of our faith. Trusting God isn't about evading difficulties, but facing them with an unwavering belief that trials hold a purpose. It's during these trials that our faith deepens, fortifying us to endure with hope and patience.

6. Gratitude and Seeking Guidance

Trusting God cultivates gratitude—a profound recognition of blessings amidst challenges. Seeking guidance through prayer, meditation, or sacred texts becomes a channel to strengthen this trust, fostering a deeper connection to the divine.

Harmony of Trust and Responsibility

7. Balancing Faith and Action:

Trusting in God doesn't absolve us of personal responsibility. It's about harmonizing faith with action, making decisions while seeking guidance. This balance ensures an active participation in shaping our lives while staying aligned with a higher purpose.

8. Acceptance and Patience

Having faith in God nurtures acceptance—a serene acknowledgment that certain facets of life unfold in their own time. Patience blossoms from this acceptance, allowing us to embrace the present without resentment towards what's beyond our control.

After separating from my ex-husband in 2018, I began looking for a new home the following year. I decided to look for townhomes because I didn't want to cut grass or be responsible for any outside upkeep. I would often say, "I just want to pull in my garage and shut the door!" I had never cut grass and I didn't want to start now. No matter how many times I repeated this sentiment, God clearly had other plans. One day on my way to take my daughter to school, a small voice whispered, "Look at that house." Look at what house? I thought to myself. Mind you, the house being suggested was a four-bedroom house with no garage on over a half-acre lot!! What was I going to do with that house?

In spite of my thoughts, I pulled into the driveway as a few of the loose river rocks bounced against the undercarriage of my car. Once on the property, I noticed a dumpster and a shiny black pickup truck, which belonged to one of the owners. A gentleman came out of the side door and I asked if he was planning to sell the house. He said they were getting it cleaned out to list it as we speak. I asked if I could go look inside and he said, "Of course!"

As I walked up to the house, I couldn't help but notice how rickety the steps were leading to the side entrance. However, once we got inside the house, it was in immaculate condition. The house was built in 1920, but the decor looked like it was straight from 1945. It had hardwood floors throughout with a honey oak finish. There was a spiral staircase that ran from the kitchen to the basement that served as an office for the two married couples that owned it for the past 10 years. Turns out the owners were all physical therapists, but they were ready for a transition. After being pleasantly surprised by the condition of the 100-year-old brick house; I gave the guy my number on a post it note and continued my day.

A few weeks past and I still had not received a call from the man at the house. At this point, I was intrigued. Could I actually get that house and rehab it like I wanted to do for so many years? I was taking my daughter to school when I noticed that same pickup truck in the driveway. I pulled into the driveway and waited for the guy to appear again. "Hey there," I said. "Do you remember me from a few weeks ago? I gave you a post it with my number on it." He said, "I do remember! I've been looking everywhere for that post it and I cannot find it anywhere!" We talked briefly and I asked him how much he was looking to get for the house. He said he was talking to investors about $130k or $135k. At that moment, I gave him my business card and told him I was extremely interested in buying his house. The townhouses I looked at were on little to no land and they were starting at more than $142k and still needed about $20k in repairs!!

The more time that passed, the more I realized this house might just be meant for me. As I continued along the home buying process. I was met with one hurdle after the next. I had to pay off a debt, show a certain amount in savings, and the final hurdle was to bring $27,000 to the closing table. The $27,000 was to pay a shared tax debt from my failed marriage and a credit card balance, but I started to wonder if

I needed to reconsider. I prayed to God and asked Him for clarity. I said, "God if it's meant for me to buy this house, make everything go through by midnight tonight." At that point, I was still waiting for the loan approval and the response from the sellers. I received the loan approval that day and then at 11:57 p.m., I received the approval of the $135k offer from the sellers. I've never been so sure I was in God's will than I felt in that very moment.

Conclusion: The Depths and Peace in Trust

Trusting God isn't a one-size-fits-all solution, but a beacon of comfort for many navigating the complexities of life. It's about finding peace amid chaos, strength amidst vulnerabilities, and purpose in moments of doubt. Ultimately, it's a deeply personal journey—a leap of faith that unveils the profound beauty of life's mysteries.

Trusting in God transcends religious affiliations; it's a profound connection to the infinite, an embrace of the mysteries that define our existence. It offers solace in turmoil, strength in vulnerability, and purpose in uncertainty. Ultimately, it's a journey that leads to a deeper understanding of life's enigmatic beauty and the serenity found in trust.

CHAPTER
Eight

Transforming Pain into Purpose

Pain, in its myriad forms, often feels like an unwelcome guest in our lives. Yet, within the depths of our struggles lies an incredible potential—to transform that pain into a powerful driving force, a catalyst for finding profound purpose and meaning.

Understanding Pain's Potential

• *Acknowledging the Depths of Pain:* Pain arrives in diverse guises—emotional, physical, or spiritual. It's an intrinsic part of the human experience. Understanding the depth of our pain is the first step towards harnessing its transformative power.

• *Reshaping Perspectives:* Pain need not be an endpoint, but a turning point. It holds within it the seeds of transformation, urging us to seek purpose amidst the turmoil. It's a call to explore the lessons hidden within the depths of suffering.

Embracing the Journey

• *Unveiling Resilience:* Adversity often unveils our inner strength. Turning pain into purpose is a testament to resilience—a conscious decision to rise despite the challenges, harnessing the energy from within to propel us forward.

• *Finding Meaning Amidst Chaos:* Within the chaos of pain lies an opportunity to discover meaning. It's about introspection, seeking the silver linings amidst the darkest clouds. Pain's purpose emerges when we channel it into a force that serves not only ourselves but others.

Navigating the Transformation

• *Healing and Growth:* Healing isn't erasing pain; it's evolving beyond it. It's a journey of growth, where pain becomes a teacher, guiding us towards empathy, wisdom, and a deeper understanding of ourselves and others.

• *Empathy and Compassion:* Pain fosters empathy—a profound understanding of others' struggles. As we transform our own pain, we cultivate compassion, becoming a source of strength and support for those enduring similar paths.

Cultivating Purpose

• *Purposeful Actions:* Channeling pain into purpose involves taking deliberate actions. It's about using our experiences to drive positive change—whether through creative endeavors, advocacy, or supporting causes close to our hearts.

• *Legacy of Transformation:* Turning pain into purpose isn't solely for personal growth; it leaves an enduring legacy. It's about inspiring others by showcasing resilience, courage, and the transformative power of turning adversity into a force for good.

Understanding the Depths of Pain

1. Diverse Forms of Pain:

Pain is an intricate tapestry woven from various threads—loss, trauma, heartache, and adversity. Its manifestations are diverse, spanning emotional, physical, and spiritual realms. Acknowledging this complexity is crucial to unraveling its transformative power.

2. Shifting Perspectives:

Pain isn't a stagnant pool but a crossroads—an opportunity to shift perspectives. It's about reframing our experiences, viewing them not as mere sources of anguish but as catalysts for growth and purpose.

Embracing the Journey of Transformation

3. Resilience Amidst Adversity:

Adversity unfurls our resilience, summoning inner strength we never knew existed. Transforming pain into purpose involves a conscious decision to rise despite the challenges, harnessing this resilience to propel us forward.

4. Finding Meaning in the Chaos:

Purpose emerges from the depths of chaos. It's an excavation process, seeking meaning within the turmoil. It involves introspection, extracting lessons from pain and using these insights to craft a meaningful narrative.

Navigating the Transformational Process

5. Healing and Growth:

Healing isn't erasing the scars; it's embracing them as part of our narrative. Transformative growth occurs when pain becomes a catalyst for self-discovery and personal evolution.

6. Empathy and Compassion:

Pain fosters empathy—a profound understanding of others' struggles. As we transform our own pain, we cultivate compassion, becoming a beacon of support for those navigating similar paths.

7. Purposeful Actions:

Channeling pain into purpose involves deliberate actions. It's about using our experiences to drive positive change—be it through advocacy, creative expression, or supporting causes aligned with our values.

8. Legacy of Transformation:

Transforming pain into purpose transcends personal growth; it leaves an enduring legacy. It's about inspiring others through resilience, showcasing that pain need not define us but can fuel our journey toward purpose and positive change.

As far back as I can remember, I always knew losing my mother at such a young age would be a defining moment in my life. Most people I knew had not experienced the death of a parent. Some of my friends had grandparents that passed, but it was rare to meet someone that lost a parent, especially a mother. By the age of ten, I had two friends that lost their mothers. One was, Barbara Sue, a Caucasian girl that lived next door to me on Luray Court. She and her brother lived with their mee-maw and paw paw. Their mom died from carbon monoxide poison in the garage before they reached school age. The other friend who lost her mom was a no nonsense little Black girl that went to school with me at Lincoln Heights Elementary. Her name was Tyanna and her mom died from cancer just a few years before I moved to Cincinnati.

After leaving Louisville, I never saw Barbara Sue again. I spent many of my days up to the age of ten going on adventures with Barbara Sue. Barbara Sue, Ellie Margaret, Ian, and I played various games in the cul-de-sac. No shoes, sometimes no shirt, no problem! It was Kentucky after all. It was a different time back then and Kentucky had a way of making you feel like the world was your oyster.

The lives of Barbara Sue and Tyanna had a similar start and unfortunately, I can't say how they progressed. I lost touch with both over the years. Our lives just went in completely different directions. While it was comforting to know I wasn't the only one to lose my mother at a young age, I couldn't let losing my mother define me. As I grew older, I decided to take back my life and no longer live in fear of meeting the same fate of passing away prematurely. Because my mother died at thirty-two years old, I felt like there may was some sort of omen on my life and I too would meet our maker at an early age. I spent years not wanting to do anything that resembled my mother's life. I didn't want to be a teacher or pledge a sorority and I avoided semi-trucks because I always thought that she was hit head on by a semi. She was not hit by a semi-truck. She ran into a small pickup truck, but there were multiple cars involved in the fatal car accident.

The car that was possibly the catalyst for it all

may not have been photographed at the scene. But that doesn't mean the damage hasn't been done. No one would ever argue that my sister and I didn't have the right to feel sorry for ourselves. That we might even have reason not to trust God. In the end, we all have choices. Feel sorry for ourselves or be resilient. Trust God or live in fear and lastly, become a victim of our circumstances or take the pain and turn it into purpose. I choose to be resilient, trust God, and find purpose in what I have gone through. My life is a walking billboard for how to turn pain into purpose and I wouldn't have it any other way!

Conclusion: Embracing Transformation

Turning pain into purpose isn't a swift or linear process; it's a tapestry woven with intricate threads of resilience, introspection, and empathy. It's about embracing the metamorphosis that pain catalyzes, discovering meaning within the chaos, and emerging as a beacon of hope—both for ourselves and for those who tread similar paths. In this transformation, pain becomes not a burden, but a profound catalyst for purpose and positive change. I always say, we are not qualified to lead people out of a situation until we have endured that situation for ourselves. Once you have gone through a certain experience, it is easier to navigate the twists and turns that come with conquering the highs and lows that come with it.

The ability to transform your pain into purpose is a profound journey that transcends the mere acknowledgment of suffering; it's a conscious decision to harness the transformative potential hidden within our deepest struggles. This transformation isn't a swift or linear process; it's a journey marked by resilience, introspection, and empathy. It involves transforming the anguish into a force for good, both for ourselves and for the world around us. In this metamorphosis, pain ceases to be a burden; it becomes a powerful catalyst propelling us towards profound purpose and inspiring others to embark on their transformative journeys.

CHAPTER
Nine

Honoring Her Legacy

Many may be wondering why I would want to write a book about the death of my mother. I was compelled to write this book to give my mother a voice and to encourage people not to be silenced by anyone or anything. We all have a purpose here on earth and the days we are given should be cherished, but most importantly leveraged to leave something behind. The stories in these pages are my attempt at correcting the wrongs in my life so that someone else can live their truth out loud and in full color.

We've all experienced childhood trauma. It may not be as severe as losing a parent, but it still affects our world just the same. A traumatic event takes place in our lives and forever changes our perspective. It's not so much what we've gone through, but how we respond to it.

Becoming a victim to our trauma makes us powerless, but embracing our trauma to help someone else makes us superheroes.

Take stock of what you've gone through and seek to understand why you were chosen for that lesson in life. How have you been equipped to endure the battle wounds that were sent your way? What have your battle wounds prepared you for in this lifetime? How can you ensure the lessons live on beyond your days here on earth? Don't think about what your parents would do, what your friends would do, or various family members. Listen to your own intuition. Gather your thoughts on your own experiences, your own perspective of what your life is meant to become, and how it was supposed to unfold for the highest good. Who are the people you are meant to lead? What is the lesson you are meant to teach? Big or small you are here on purpose, for a purpose.

I used to think of what I would want people to say at my funeral, but that seemed a bit morbid. As a result, I decided to elevate my expectations and think about what I would want my grandchildren and great grandchildren to say about me. How would I want them to light up speaking of the legacy I left for them? I want them to speak about the land I left for each of them so that they could in turn do the same for their children. That I provided them with a manual on how to live life to the fullest and leave a legacy behind for those that followed. And that life is not about what happens to you, but instead how you respond to whatever that thing is.

I often think of what would have been different had my mother not passed away on that fateful day in 1983. Because I'm a realist, it's not all flowers and rainbows. Sometimes I think of the possibility that my life could have been worse if my mother lived. Not for the fact that she would have been our primary caregiver, but the thought that we may have lived in fear. Fear that one day our father's wrath would turn to us. I am not sure my mother would have ever worked up the nerve to fully leave my dad. The thought of living in fear of a man beating your mother day in and day out, may not have been an adversity I could endure. It may not have been a battle wound set out for me to embody.

I also think of the people that would be absent from my life if my mother lived like my stepmother and her family. I've learned so many valuable lessons and have so many fond memories of the Bridgewater family. I can't imagine my life without them in it!

Don't get me wrong, I had my moments of daydreaming about my mother. I imagined what she would have been like, the sound of her voice, and the magnitude of her hugs. And I thought of how impactful her advice might have been for me throughout the years. While the daydreams are sweet, I'm immediately met with the sadness that comes afterward because every action has a reaction. Every time something changes about our stories, we change. I may have gone to completely different schools, had different friends, cleaved to different family members. My life would be very different and as a result, I wouldn't be who I am today.

I love who I am, who I have become in this lifetime, and I wouldn't change a thing. I'm grateful for the adversity I've faced in my life and I don't have any regrets. I don't want to rewrite any part of my story. I truly want to keep living, creating memories, and preparing the next generation to embrace the legacy left for them. In addition to them embracing their own legacy, I want them to pick up the baton and cherish what they are building to pass on to the generation to come. Our lives are not our own. Our lives are meant to be a blueprint to those coming behind us. If we aren't in position, how can we expect them to be?

I leave you with this: begin with the end in mind. In your ancestor's final days what would you have them say about you? What would you like them to remember you for? How would you want your story to be told to your great, great grandchildren? Are you living a life you would be proud to have illustrated in a book or a movie? If not, how can you change the narrative? Is there a cause you can initiate? Does your life experience qualify you to lead anyone out of darkness? Have you been abused and want to take up the fight against child abuse? Have you been bullied and want to teach others the signs of cyberbullying? Have you lost a close friend and want to start a virtual hug app? Whatever it is, it is unique to you. It's not for your sister to do, your best friend, your sorority sister, your cousin, your neighbor. What is for you, is for you!!

Start thinking about the legacy you want
to leave today.

What experience in life has the most impact on who
you have become?

_____

_____

_____

_____

_____

_____

_____

_____

_____

_____

_____

_____

Who are you in the story? Are you a victim or a victor? How can you change the dynamics? What are your superpowers and how can you activate them?

_____

_____

_____

_____

_____

_____

_____

_____

_____

_____

_____

_____

_____

_____

What do you need to believe God, the universe, Buddha, or Allah for in your life? How have you minimized your power? What are some ways to take your power back and become who you were called to be?

_____

_____

_____

_____

_____

_____

_____

_____

_____

_____

_____

_____

Who are you qualified to lead? How can their lives improve because of you?

_____

_____

_____

_____

_____

_____

_____

_____

_____

_____

_____

_____

_____

_____

_____

EPILOGUE

A Lesson in Resilience

Gail Ann's story serves as a poignant reminder of the fragility of life and the importance of addressing our emotional struggles before they escalate. It highlights the significance of seeking support and speaking out about abuse and mental health issues, breaking the silence that often surrounds these challenges.

Though her journey ended tragically, Gail Ann's memory will forever live in the hearts of those she touched. Her story becomes a beacon of resilience, inspiring others to seek help, embrace change, and build a brighter future, even in the darkest of times.

Note: It's essential to approach sensitive topics with care and respect. This story aims to shed light on the importance of addressing emotional struggles, seeking support, and raising awareness about abuse and mental health issues.

www.ingramcontent.com/pod-product-compliance
Lightning Source LLC
Chambersburg PA
CBHW071237090426
42736CB00014B/3114